MODERN CLASSIC SONATAS

—— BOOK 1 ——

DR. ANIS I. MILAD

authorHOUSE®

AuthorHouse™
1663 Liberty Drive
Bloomington, IN 47403
www.authorhouse.com
Phone: 1 (800) 839-8640

Published by AuthorHouse 06/26/2019

ISBN: 978-1-7283-1722-9 (sc)
ISBN: 978-1-7283-1721-2 (e)

Print information available on the last page.

Any people depicted in stock imagery provided by Getty Images are models, and such images are being used for illustrative purposes only. Certain stock imagery © Getty Images.

This book is printed on acid-free paper.

"This book 'Modern Classic Sonatas - Book 1' includes sonatas which were composed by Dr. Anis I. Milad. Dr. Milad expressed his emotion and was able to complete each sonata in three parts "exposition, development, and recapitulation" and in a variety of Key Signature. These sonatas are also published in YouTube. Producing books to include this form of music is a door for the new generations to follow and improve the classic music. This book is also produced to get the attention of the conductors and the musicians around the world to our world in the United States of America."

CONTENTS

Score

Sonata No 1, Op 67 - The Girl Behind the Mask

Dr. Anis I. Milad

Pno.

Vc.

Sonata No 2, Op 44 - Salwa the Lightning Goddess

Dr. Anis I. Milad

Sonata No 3, Op 46 – Within the Sun God

Dr. Anis I. Milad

Sonata No 4, Op 48 - Glancing the Future

Dr. Anis I. Milad

Sonata No 5, Op 50 - The Myth of Mortality

Dr. Anis I. Milad

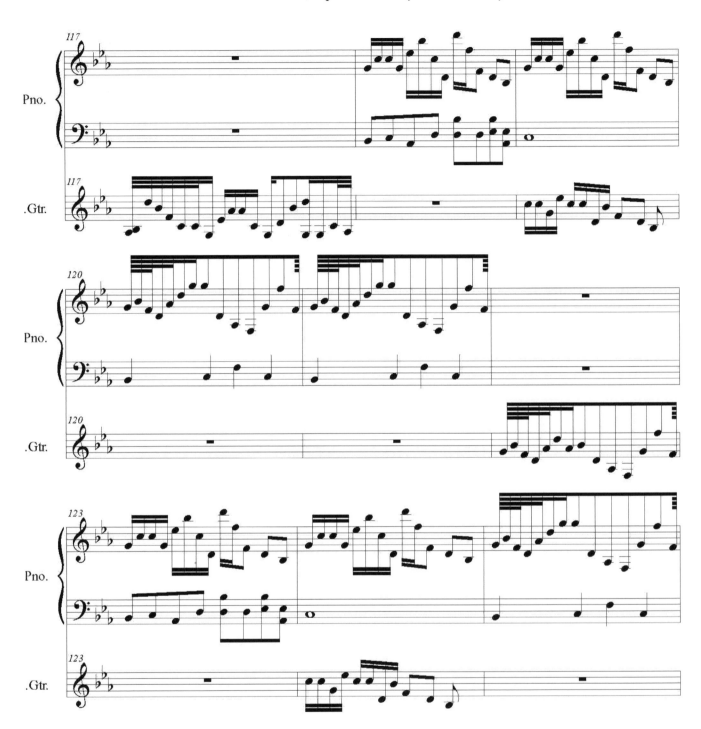

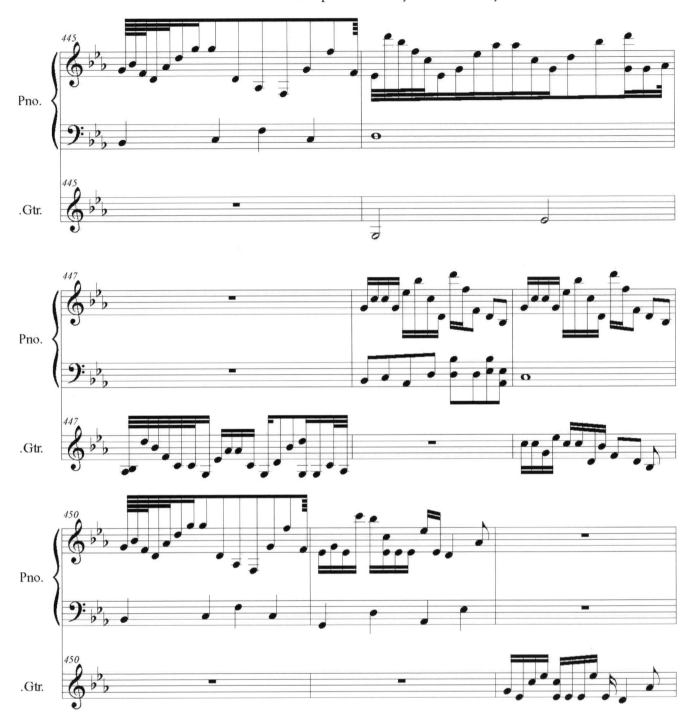

Sonata No 6, Op 52 - Reproachful Verses the Unholy

Dr. Anis I. Milad

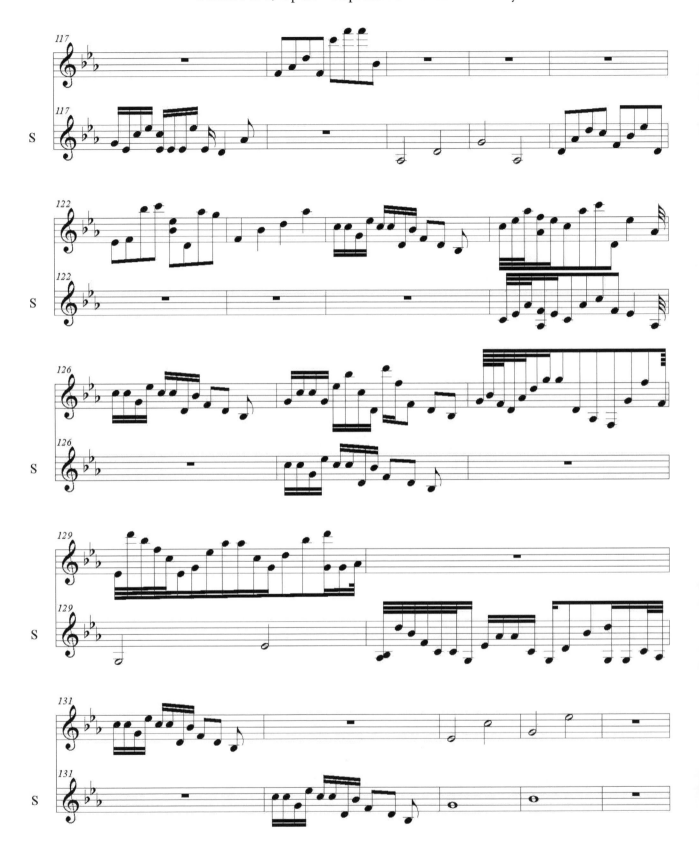

Sonata No 7, Op 54 - Expression of Sorrow for Lost Peace

Dr. Anis I. Milad

Sonata No 8, Op 56 - Paris My Delightful City

Dr. Anis I. Milad

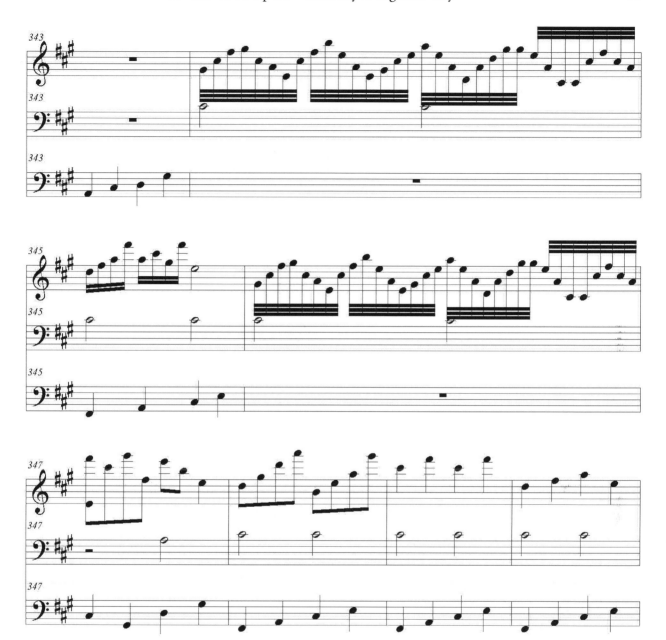

Sonata No 9, Op 58 - Lauren My Wildest Dream

Dr. Anis I. Milad

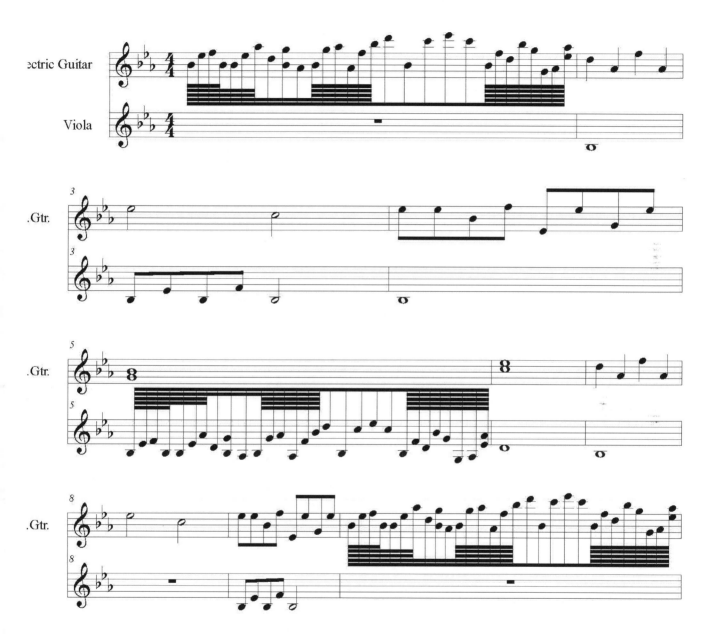

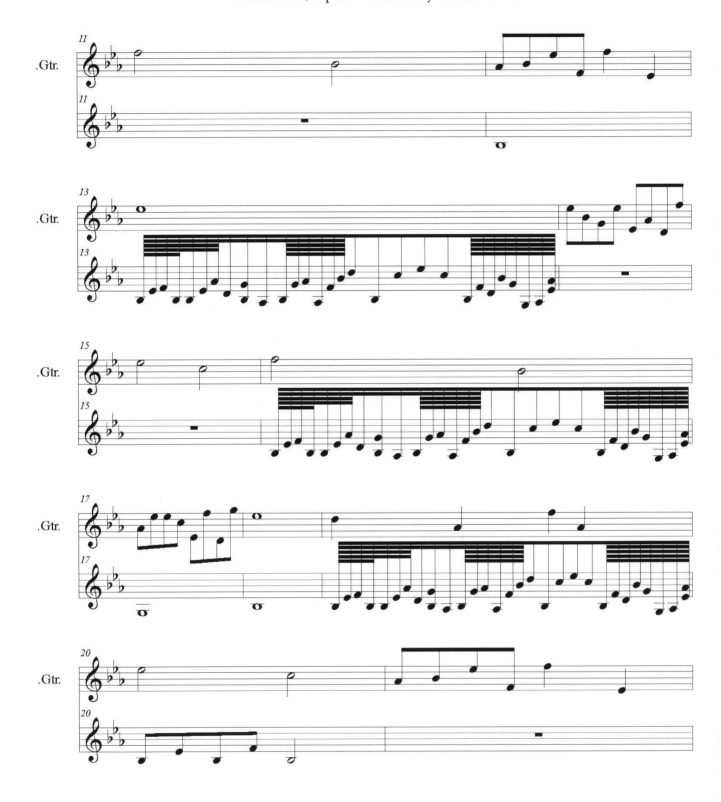

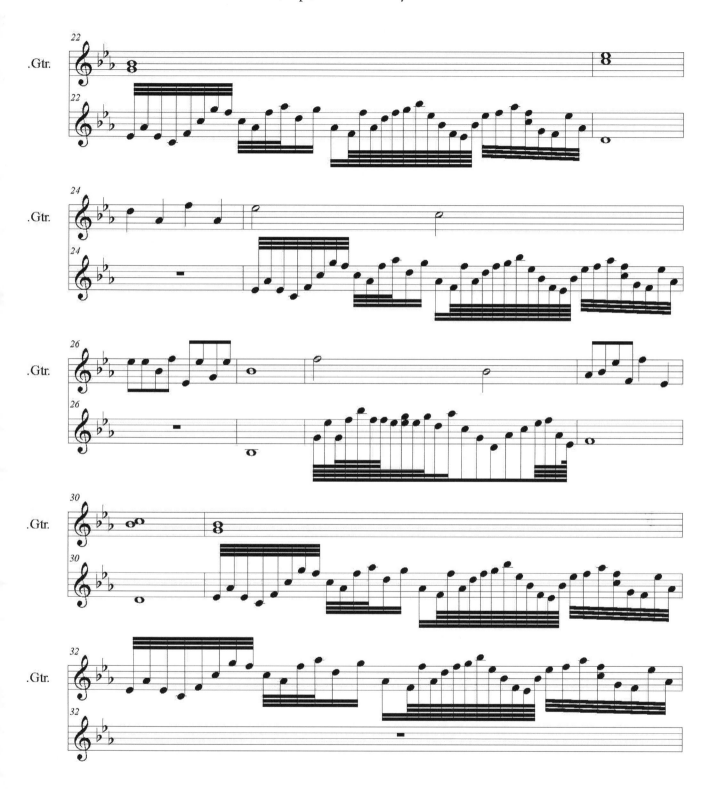

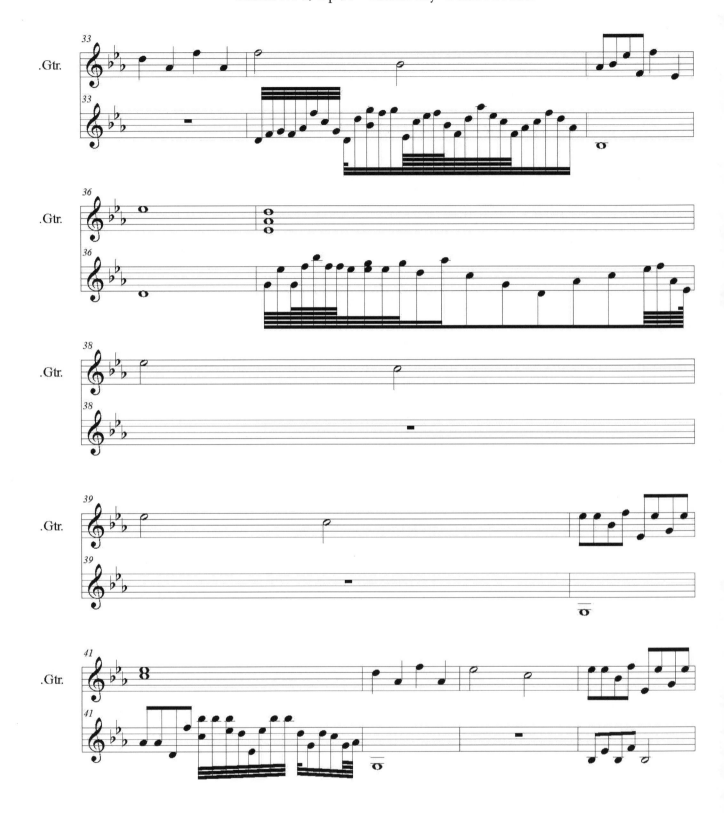

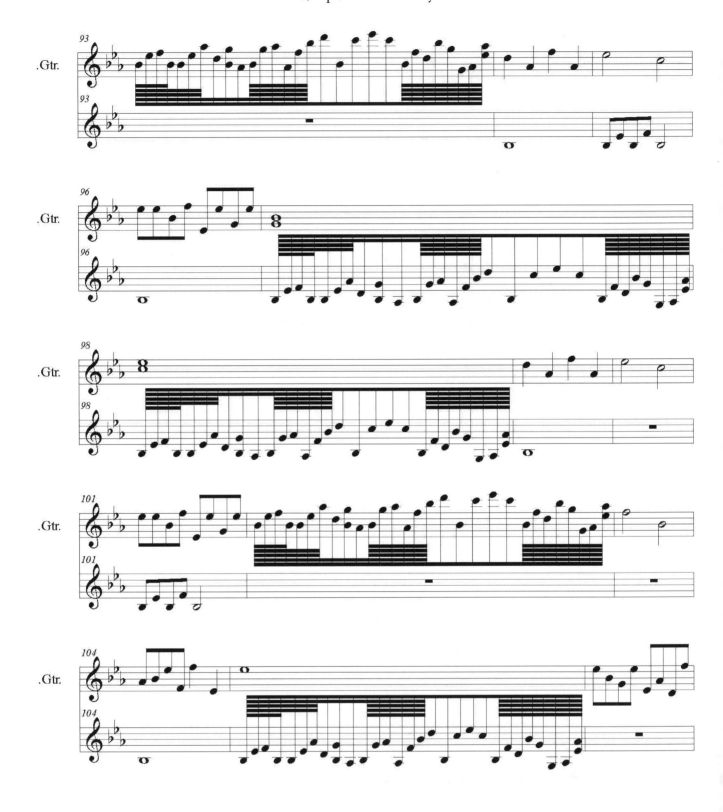

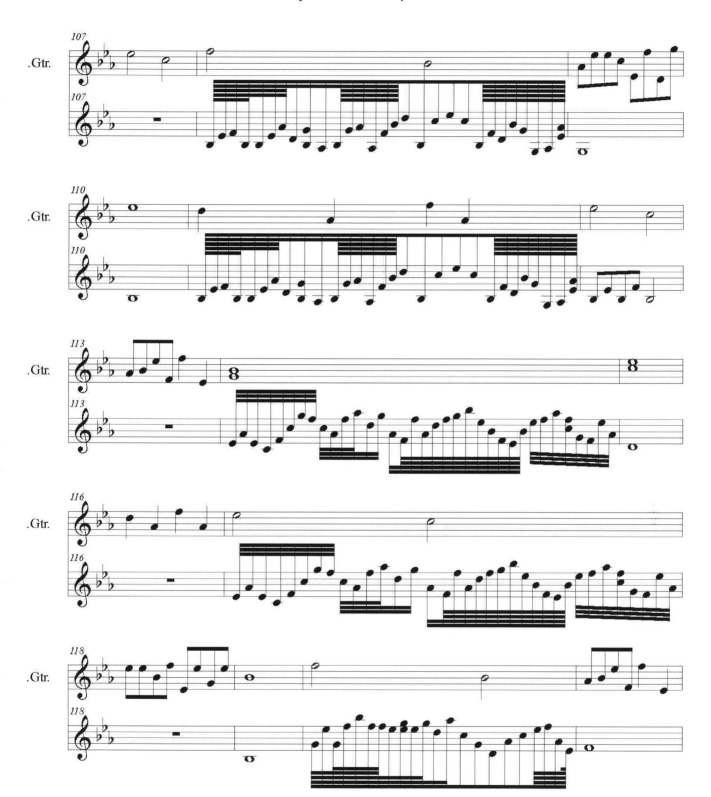

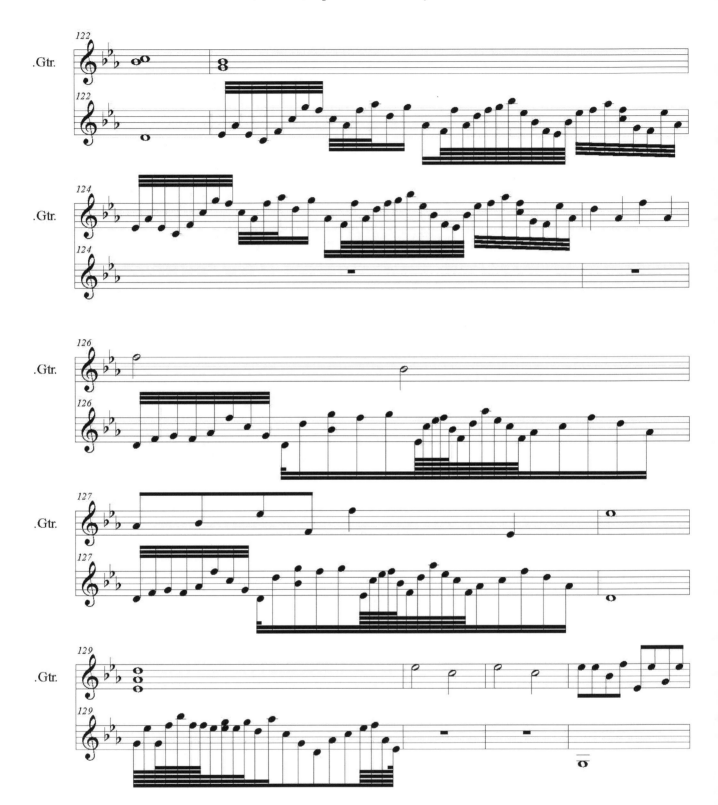

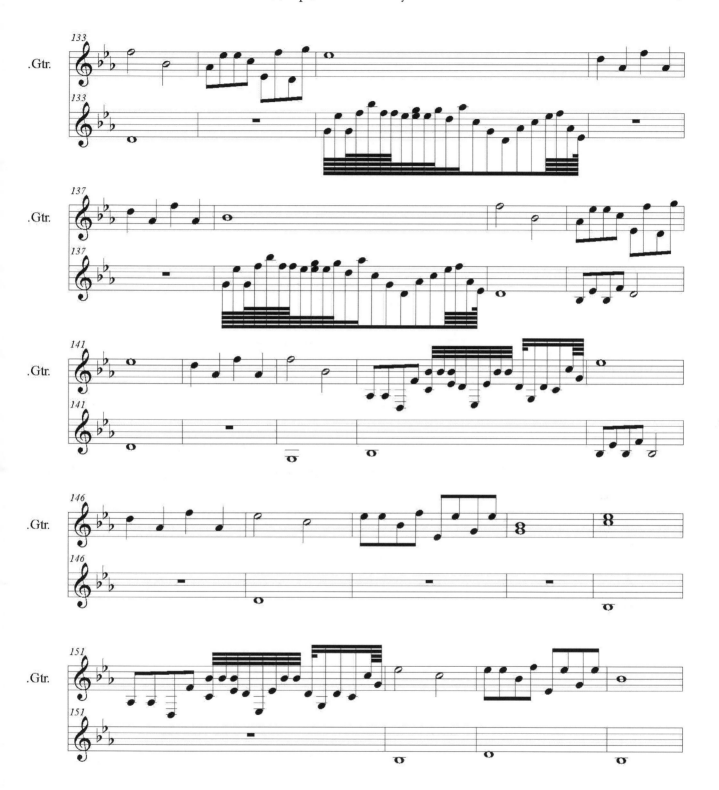

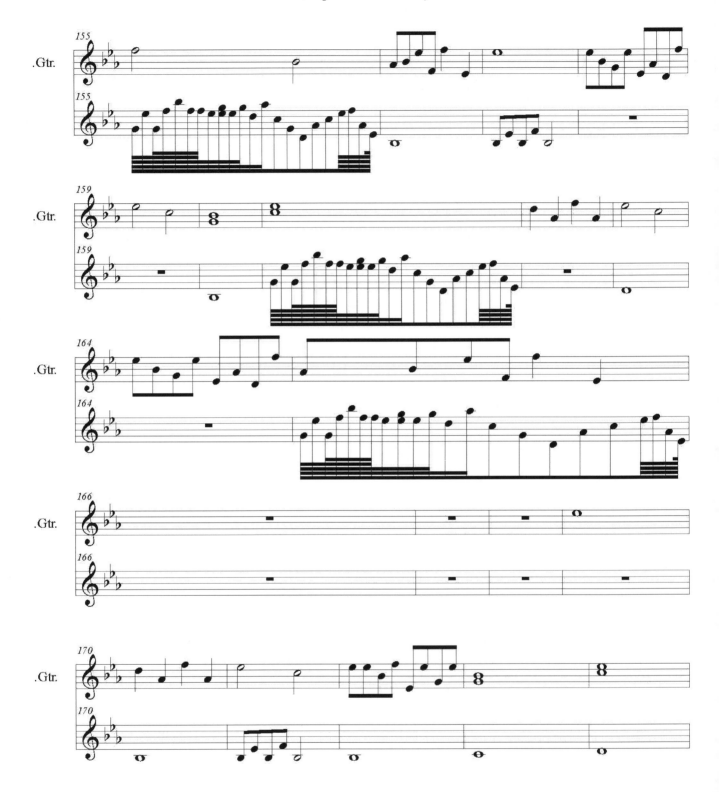

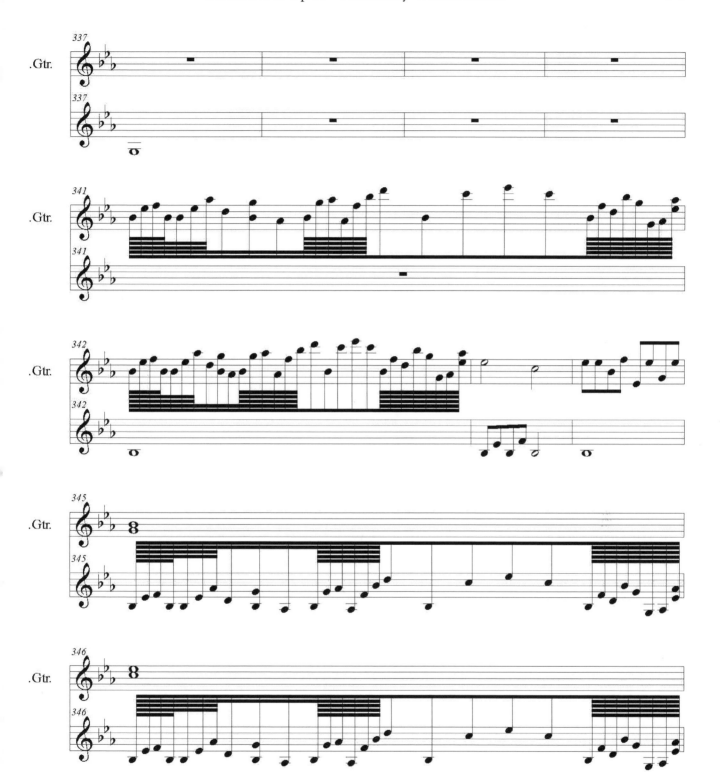

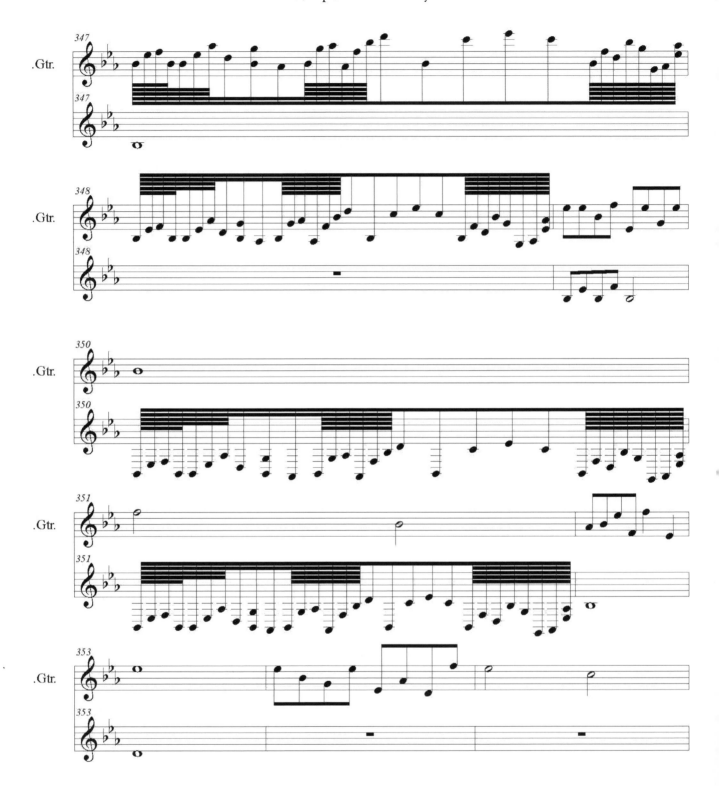

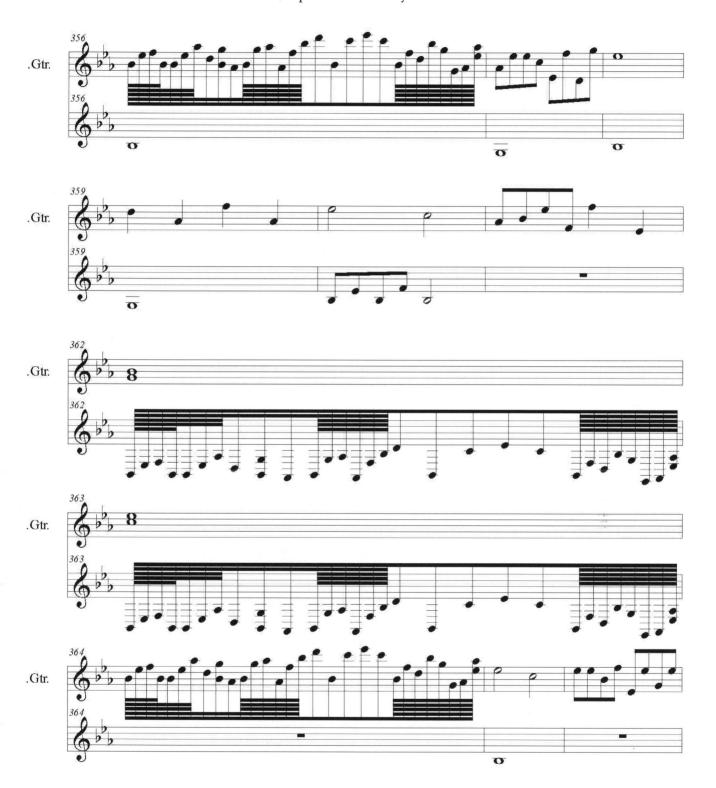

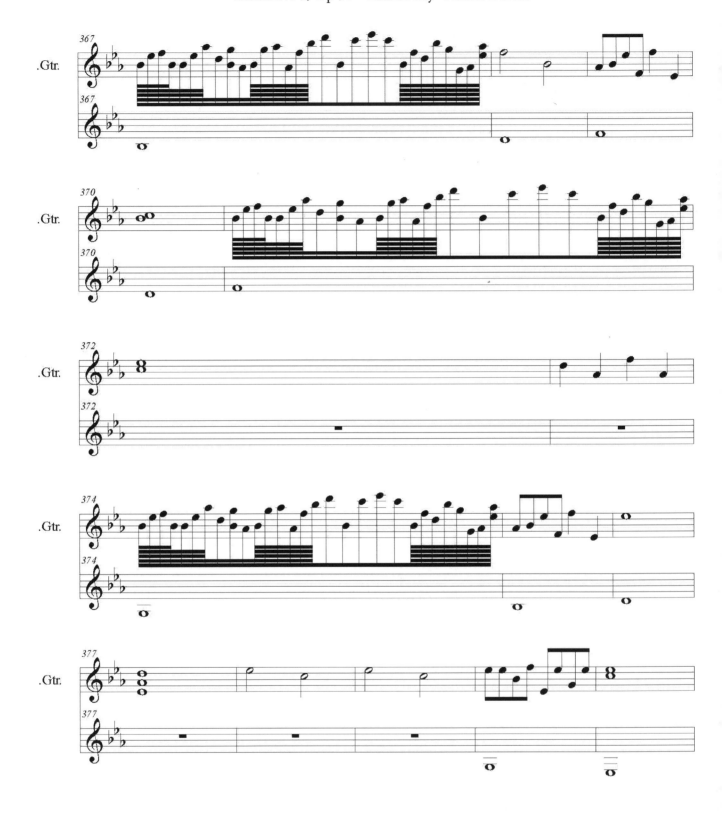

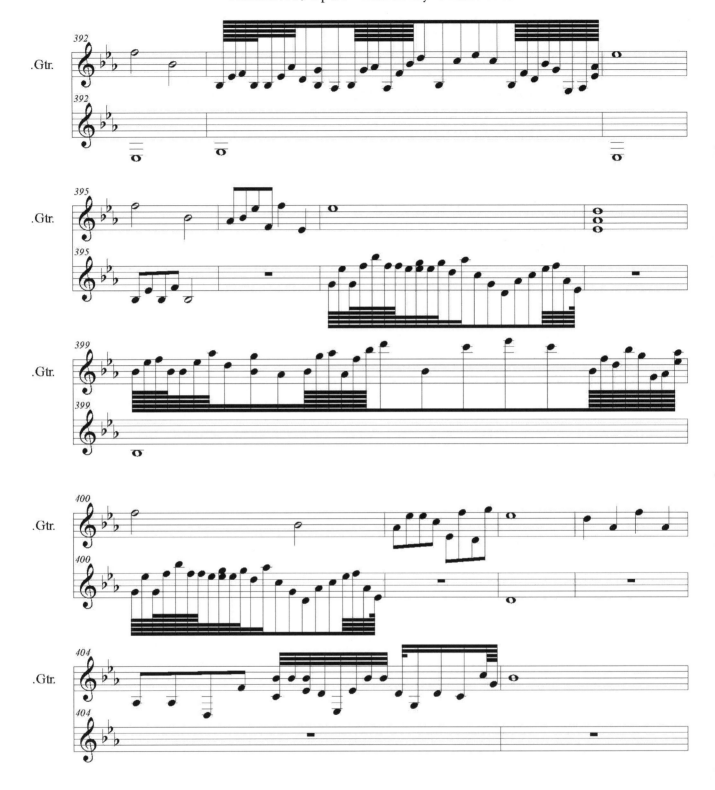

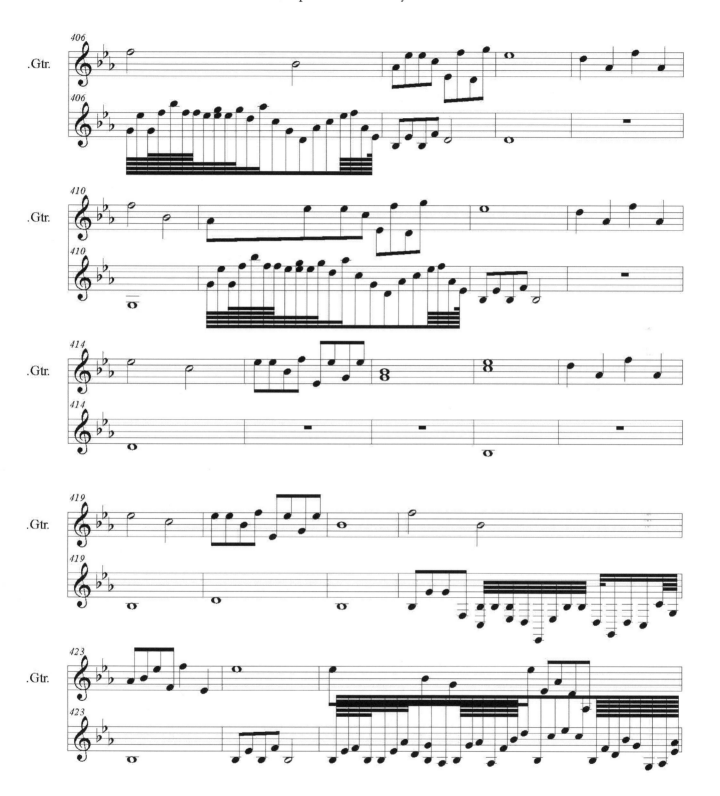

Sonata No 10, Op 60 - My Daughter the Eternal Mirage

Dr. Anis I. Milad